The Science of Living Things

# what is a Bird?

## A Bobbie Kalman Book

Crabtree Publishing Company

www.crabtreebooks.com

# The Science of Living Things Series
## A Bobbie Kalman Book

**To my mom, Ursula Sotzek,
who helped me spread my wings and fly!**

**Author and Editor-in-Chief**
Bobbie Kalman

**Managing editor**
Lynda Hale

**Research and editing team**
April Fast
Heather Levigne
Kate Calder

**Computer design**
Lynda Hale

**Production coordinator
  and photo researcher**
Hannelore Sotzek

**Special thanks to**
Ron Rohrbaugh, Assistant Director of Education,
Cornell Laboratory of Ornithology

**Photographs**
Gene Boaz: back cover, pages 13 (left), 22
Russell C. Hansen: page 29
James Kamstra: page 18
David Liebman: page 26
Robert McCaw: page 20 (top)
Photo Researchers, Inc.: Stephen Dalton: page 17; Tim Davis: page23 (bottom);
    Kenneth W. Fink/NAS: page 13 (right); Fletcher & Baylis: page 28;
    Tom & Pat Leeson: page 25 (bottom); Craig K. Lorenz: page 23 (top);
    Renee Lynn: pages 19 (top right), 23 (middle); Tom McHugh: pages 15,
    19 (bottom); Millard H. Sharp: page 30; Helen Williams pages 19 (top left),
James H. Robinson: title page, pages 7 (bottom), 12, 20 (bottom), 21 (right)
James P. Rowan: pages 21 (left), 25 (top)
Other photographs by Digital Stock and Digital Vision

**Illustrations**
Barbara Bedell: pages 4-5, 7, 14 (top), 27, 28, 29
Antoinette "Cookie" Bortolon: page 25
Bonna Rouse: pages 9, 11, 16-17
Doug Swinamer: pages 12, 14 (bottom)

## Crabtree Publishing Company

www.crabtreebooks.com       1-800-387-7650

**Cataloging in Publication Data**
Kalman, Bobbie
    What is a bird?
(The science of living things)
Includes index.
ISBN 0-86505-880-6 (library bound)   ISBN 0-86505-892-X (pbk.)
This book introduces birds, describing some different types and
discussing their physical characteristics, behaviors, and habitats.
1. Birds—Juvenile literature. [1. Birds.] I. Kalman, Bobbie. II. Series:
Kalman, Bobbie. Science of living things.

QL676.2.W485 1999               j598               LC 98-30911
                                                              CIP

**Published in
the United States**

PMB16A
350 Fifth Ave.
Suite 3308
New York, NY
10118

**Published
in Canada**

616 Welland Ave.,
St. Catharines, Ontario
Canada
L2M 5V6

**Published in the
United Kingdom**

73 Lime Walk
Headington
Oxford
OX3 7AD
United Kingdom

**Published
in Australia**

386 Mt. Alexander Rd.,
Ascot Vale (Melbourne)
VIC 3032

# Contents

# What is a bird?

A bird is an animal that has a beak, two legs, two wings, and feathers. There are 9000 different **species**, or kinds, of birds. Most birds fly, but there are some that do not. Some birds, such as hummingbirds, are tiny. Others, such as ostriches, are huge.

Birds can be found in forests, deserts, and grasslands. Many birds live on water. A few birds make icy, cold places their home. Name some birds that you know.

*toucan*

*quetzal*

*Rainforest birds such as the toucan and quetzal have colorful beaks and feathers.*

*cassowary*

*penguin*

## A bird…
- is an animal with wings.
- has a beak and feathers.
- has a backbone.
- is warm-blooded. Its body temperature stays the same in both warm and cold surroundings.

*Not all birds fly! Birds such as the emu, ostrich, and cassowary do not fly. They have strong legs for running. The penguin is another flightless bird. Millions of years ago, the penguin's flippers were wings. Now its flippers are used for swimming instead of flying.*

4

The green woodpecker and the cardinal are **perching birds** that make their homes in trees. A woodpecker carves its nest into the tree itself! Other perching birds build nests of grasses and twigs.

green woodpecker

cardinal

secretary bird

barn owl

**Raptors** eat other animals. They are hunters that use their feet to catch prey. The secretary bird and the barn owl are raptors.

flamingo

wood duck

crab plover

**Ground-dwelling birds** such as the red grouse and chicken are able to fly, but they do not fly often. These birds have adapted to life on the ground. They eat seeds, fruit, and insects.

The flamingo, wood duck, and crab plover are **water birds**. Water birds live on ponds, swamps, wetlands, lakes, and oceans. They eat small fish, worms, and plants that they find on the bottom.

red grouse

5

# A bird's body

The body of most birds is suited to flying. In order to fly, birds must be lightweight. Hollow bones help make their bodies light. The **streamlined**, or sleek, shape of a bird's body also helps a bird fly. It allows the bird to glide easily through the air.

A bird uses its nostrils to breathe and smell. Most birds do not have a strong sense of smell.

Birds have lungs for breathing air.

Birds that fly have strong chest muscles that help them flap their wings.

The bird uses its feet for perching on trees, gathering food, and walking or swimming.

The tail helps the bird steer when it is flying.

*Birds that do not fly, such as this rhea, have small wings and weak chest muscles. The rhea belongs to the **ratite** family. Emus, kiwis, ostriches, and cassowaries are other ratites. Ratites are flightless birds. Many have a long neck and large eyes to help them spot predators from far away. They have strong legs for running fast and big bones for holding up their heavy body.*

Birds use their beak for gathering and eating food. They have no teeth, so their head is light.

A bird uses its wings for taking off, gliding, soaring, and landing.

Birds can see color. Most birds have eyes on the sides of their head to see things all around them. An owl's eyes face forward, like ours, to help them spot prey from high in the air.

# All about beaks

All birds have beaks. Beaks are also known as bills. They come in many shapes and sizes. Birds use their beak for catching or breaking apart food. Some birds also use their beak for making nests.

## What is in a beak?

Beaks are made of light, hard bone. They are covered with layers of **keratin**. Keratin is a hard material from which animal horns and hoofs are made. Our nails are also made of keratin.

*The pelican's long beak has an enormous sac of skin on the bottom bill for catching fish. The pelican swallows fish without chewing them.*

Common bee-eaters have a long, narrow beak that is perfect for quickly catching flying insects—especially bees! The bird rubs the bee against a tree to remove its stinger.

Fruit and seed-eating birds, such as the parrot, have a strong, curved beak. They use their beak to pierce the tough skin of fruit and crack open fruit pits and seeds.

*bee-eater*

*parrot*

Eagles are raptors. Their beak is curved and has a sharp hook for tearing apart prey.

*eagle*

*avocet*

*swan*

The avocet is a wading bird that walks into shallow water to feed. Many wading birds have a long, thin beak for probing into the sand or mud to find shellfish or insect larvae.

Swans and ducks have flat, broad beaks. They swim in shallow water. They put their head underwater to scoop up small animals and grab plants from the muddy bottom.

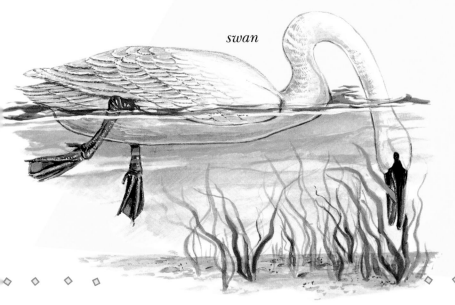

9

# Feet facts

Birds use their feet in many ways. Some use them to catch food. Others build nests with their feet. Many water birds have webbed feet for swimming.

Most birds have four toes on each foot. Three toes face forward, and one faces backward. The heel is located above the toes. It looks like a backward knee, but the bird's real knee is close to its body, under its feathers.

Birds such as this cape weaver can sleep on a high tree branch by **perching**! To perch, a bird wraps its clawlike feet around a branch and crouches down.

Raptors have **talons**, or sharp, curved feet with claws. They use their talons to hit and grab their prey. Raptors can also use their strong feet to hold an animal while they eat it.

*The ostrich is the fastest running bird because of its large, strong feet and long legs.*

Birds that live near water and eat fish have webbed feet. A flap of skin connects their toes. They use their webbed feet to paddle through the water. By using their feet like flippers, they can dive deep to catch fish.

Most birds sit on their eggs to keep them warm. Some warm their eggs with their feet. The booby spreads its large webbed feet over its eggs.

*The African jacana has long toes that help spread out its body weight. Jacanas can walk on lily pads without sinking!*

11

# Only birds have feathers

Birds are the only animals on earth that have feathers. There are two main types of feathers—**down** and **contour**. Down feathers are soft and fluffy. They are close to the body and keep the bird warm. The contour, or outer, feathers are smooth and stiff. They cover the down feathers and keep the bird dry. Contour feathers give birds their sleek, streamlined shape.

## Flight feathers

Flight feathers are the contour feathers on the bird's wing and tail. The small flight feathers close tightly when the bird wants to fly higher. The large ones allow the bird to change direction.

*This spoonbill is using its beak to **preen**, or smooth and clean, its feathers.*

shaft

barbules

*Contour feathers have tiny parts called **barbules** that lock together in the same way zippers do, making the feathers waterproof.*

## A change of clothing

Old feathers get dirty and worn out. They **molt**, or fall out, and new ones grow in their place. Depending on the season, the new feathers may be a different color than the old ones. The ptarmigan, a bird that lives in the Arctic, loses its brown feathers in the fall and grows white ones to blend in with the winter snow.

## Colorful creatures

Many birds have colorful feathers and markings that allow them to blend in with their habitat. The colors and markings **camouflage**, or hide, the bird so its predators cannot see it.

*(right) Some birds attract mates with their colorful feathers. The male Lady Amherst's pheasant has bright red, yellow, and blue feathers that it ruffles and displays to attract a female.*

*(left) A ptarmigan's feathers are white in winter to camouflage the bird in its snowy home.*

13

# Why do birds fly?

Scientists believe that birds were reptiles millions of years ago. Some reptiles **evolved**, or changed, in order to survive. They grew flaps of skin between their front and hind legs and used these flaps to glide from tree to tree. In time, these flaps became feather-covered wings. It took millions of years, but these ancient reptiles learned to fly. They became birds.

*bird with tail feathers*

*reptile with wings*

*ancient reptile with skin flaps*

*ancient reptile*

## Quick getaways and long trips

Birds fly to avoid predators. They can escape a hungry cat, weasel, rat, or human by flying away quickly. Birds also fly to **migrate** to different areas when the seasons change. They spend the spring and summer in one area and move to a warmer place when the weather turns cold.

## Flying for food

Birds fly to escape predators and to migrate, but the main reason they fly is to find food. Flying helps birds easily spot a meal from the sky. Some birds glide over lakes and oceans in search of fish. Flying allows many birds to reach the tops of tall trees where they can feast on fruit and seeds.

*Bald eagles fly to the tops of trees where they have a good view for spotting prey on the ground below.*

# The art of flying

Birds use many parts of their body for flying. Their tail, feathers, muscles, legs, and feet all play an important role. The four main stages of flight are taking off, flapping, soaring and gliding, and landing.

A bird's wing is specially designed to use the air as it flies. By moving its wings in the air, a bird can take off, soar, turn, slow down, and land.

*In order to fly, birds must push against the air with their wings. This pushing up and down is called **flapping**. When they are about to take off, birds flap their wings quickly. Air moving over and under the wings helps lift the bird off the ground.*

*Birds continue flapping to carry them high up into the air. They have strong chest muscles that help push their wings up and down.*

## Going nowhere fast!

Hummingbirds flap their wings very quickly in order to **hover,** or stay in one place. They flap them so quickly, their wings seem to disappear! Flying without moving from place to place takes a lot of energy.

*Once a bird is in the air, it does not need to flap constantly. Flying is tiring work that takes a lot of energy. Sometimes birds save energy by gliding and soaring. They stretch out their wings and let the wind carry them along.*

*When a bird is ready to land, it seems to stand up in midair. Air pushing against its body slows down the bird. It "puts on the brakes" by tilting its wings back to push against the air. The bird then spreads its tail feathers. As it slows down and comes near the ground, the bird stretches out its legs and lands on its feet. Birds have to be very careful. They can get injured if they hit the ground too hard!*

# Birds that cannot fly

There are over twenty kinds of birds that cannot fly. Millions of years ago, most birds had to fly to survive. They flew to find food and avoid predators. Some, however, lived in areas where they could easily find food on the ground. These habitats also had fewer predators. Since these birds did not have to fly to survive, they flew less and less often. Eventually, they stopped flying completely.

*Cassowaries have long, strong legs and can run very fast. They are shy but fierce birds. They use their sharp claws to defend themselves against enemies.*

(above) The New Zealand kiwi's wings are so tiny that they are nearly invisible! Kiwis have an excellent sense of smell. The nostrils on the tip of their beak help them find insects in the ground. (right) Penguins spend most of their time swimming. A thick layer of **blubber**, or fat, keeps them warm in their freezing habitat. (below) The emu's long, strong legs and large feet allow it to run quickly.

Like all living things, birds get energy from food. They need energy to grow, breathe, and especially to fly. Flying uses a lot of energy, so birds must keep eating to replace the energy they use. They spend most of their time looking for food or feeding. Most birds eat a variety of foods.

## Different diets

Some birds eat seeds and nuts, and others prefer insects. Many birds, however, eat both. **Birds of prey** such as eagles, hawks, owls, and ospreys hunt animals. They eat fish, reptiles, rodents, and other birds. **Carrion**, or dead animal flesh, is also part of their diet.

*Great horned owls are night hunters. They swallow prey, such as rats, whole and spit up the bones and fur later.*

*Finches eat insects, as well as fruit, seeds, and nuts.*

## Ways of getting food

Birds get food in different ways. Herring gulls drop mussels from high in the air to shatter their shells on the rocks below. Blackbirds watch while thrushes crack open snails and then rush in to steal their meal. Skuas chase other seabirds until they drop the fish they have caught.

## Eating without teeth

Birds do not have teeth, but they have a **gizzard**, which breaks up the food they eat. Some birds swallow little bits of gravel. The rough gravel stays in the gizzard and helps grind the food.

*(right) The anhinga uses its long, sharp beak to spear a fish and then swallows its wriggling prey in one bite! (below) One of these gulls has caught some fish, and the other is trying to steal its meal.*

# Where do birds live?

Flying has helped birds move all over the world. Species of birds now live everywhere from the cold Antarctic to the tropical rainforests and everywhere in-between. Part of the reason that birds can live almost everywhere is that they easily **adapt**, or change.

The body and habits of birds adapt to suit the area in which they live. Some tropical birds are able to fly for long periods of time in search of fruit. Other types of birds have become great swimmers as well as fliers. They have learned to live on water and eat fish.

(right) Burrowing owls live in underground homes made by small animals. Sometimes the owls share a burrow with prairie dogs or other animals.

(above) King penguins live on the solid ice of the Antarctic. Ice cliffs are their only shelter from the wind.

(left) Toucans find berries, fruit, and seeds in the treetops of the rainforest. They spend almost all their life above the ground.

# Home, sweet home!

Birds build nests in which to lay eggs and raise their young. Nests keep female birds and their eggs warm and comfortable. Birds have an **instinct** to build nests. Each species is born knowing where to build its nest and which materials to use.

Birds choose a nesting area where there is plenty of food nearby, so they can feed their young easily. They build nests in places that are hard for predators to find or reach—in hedges or bushes, in tree trunks, high up in trees, and among water plants.

# Many different kinds

Birds make nests from grass, hair, branches, and spider webs. They stick the materials together with mud or chewed grasses and bark. After the nests are built, birds line them with feathers, animal fur, or snakeskin to make them comfortable.

Some birds do not build their own nest. They move into a nest made by a mammal, reptile, or other bird.

*(above) A nesting **colony** is a place where a group of birds nests together. These gannets return to their nesting colony every year at mating time.*

*(left) These great herons use large twigs for their nest. The female watches the male to make sure he makes a good nest for the eggs.*

*(below) To make a nest, tailor birds sew leaves together using plant fibers, cocoon silk, and spider webs.*

25

# Bird songs?

Birds make different sounds for many different reasons. The most familiar bird sound is song. Birds sing to attract a mate and warn other birds to stay away. Baby birds sing to beg for food. They learn how to sing by copying the sounds made by their parents and the other birds of their species. A few birds such as myna birds, mockingbirds, and starlings copy the sounds made by birds of other species. Many parrots can even copy human speech!

## Singing duets

Some male and female tropical songbirds sing **duets** at mating time. When two birds sing a duet, it often means that they have mated for life.

## Danger!

Sometimes birds sing alarm notes. Alarm notes warn other birds of danger. The American robin uses one note when it sees a hawk circling overhead and another when it sees a predator on the ground. Bird partners or flocks sing location notes to help them find one another.

# Weird tunes!

Some birds make noises that do not sound like bird songs. Identify each bird by using the clue beside it.

Woodpeckers sound as if they are drumming. The kookaburra is known as the laughing jackass because its call sounds like a donkey's bray. Snowy owls bark like dogs. Starlings can mimic the sound of a telephone ringing.

*RAT, TAT, TAT! This tree is where it's at.*

*RING! RING! RING! Can you hear me sing?*

*Ass-k me to sing, Jack, and I'll have a good laugh!*

*Woof-woof! Do you know my name? Woof-woof is my claim to fame. Woof-woof is what I sing in the dark. Woof-woof! My song is a _ _ _ _.*

# Eggs and chicks

Birds mate in order to have chicks. To mate, a male bird must attract a female of its species. Some males sing songs, whereas others show off their colorful feathers. Many, such as the blue booby, do a jaunty courting jig.

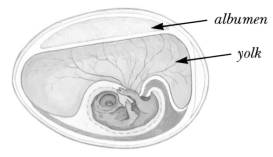

albumen

yolk

Once the birds have mated, the chicks grow in eggs that come from the mother bird's body. The **yolk** provides food for the chick. The **albumen**, or egg white, provides water and protects the chick.

boobies courting

*Most male birds such as ostriches are more colorful than the females of their species.*

# Eggs-tremely perfect!

hummingbird

robin

pheasant

tern

common loon

snowy owl

- Eggshells are made of a hard material called **calcium**.
- They have thousands of tiny holes so the chick inside can breathe.
- Eggs come in many colors and patterns to camouflage them from predators.
- Birds that live in dark places lay light-colored eggs so they can see them.
- Eggs are oval, but some are pointed at one end so they will roll in a circle and not fall to the ground.

cassowary

osprey

murre

Birds **brood**, or sit on their eggs, to keep them warm so they will hatch. Male emperor penguins brood their egg by resting it on their feet and covering it with a flap of skin called a brood pouch.

(left) The chick has an **egg tooth** on top of its beak to help it break through the shell. It makes a **pip**, or small opening, and cuts around the wide end of the egg so it can push its way out of the shell with its legs.

## Caring for chicks

Most birds are excellent parents. They give their chicks constant attention. The chicks peep and squawk for their parents to bring them insects and worms. Often their parents eat the food first. They bring it up when they return to the nest so they can carry more food home.

## Protecting the chicks

Most chicks are well camouflaged so predators cannot see them, but their parents still need to protect them. If a predator is nearby, the mother bird makes a loud noise to warn her chicks to crouch down and stay still so they will not be seen. If the predator gets too close to the chicks, the mother bird attacks it by flying towards it at a high speed.

## Warm and clean nests

Birds warm their newborn chicks with their body. If the chicks get too warm, the parents shade them with feathers, leaves, or a wing. The mother bird keeps the nest clean by pushing the eggshells and other waste out of the nest.

*Many birds feed live insects to their chicks, but the snowy egret feeds her young by bringing up food she has eaten.*

# Words to know

**albumen** The clear liquid inside an egg that provides water and protection for the growing chick; also called egg white

**barbules** Tiny parts of a feather that lock together

**blubber** A thick layer of fat under an animal's skin

**brood** To sit on eggs so they will hatch; also to sit on chicks to keep them warm

**camouflage** Colors or marks on an animal that help hide it from enemies

**contour feathers** Long, smooth feathers that cover most of a bird's body

**down feathers** The soft feathers between a bird's skin and its contour feathers

**energy** The power needed to do things

**evolve** To change or develop slowly over time

**gizzard** The part of a bird's stomach that helps grind up food

**gliding** The act of holding wings out straight and floating on the wind

**habitat** The natural place where a plant or animal is found

**hovering** The act of flapping wings quickly and staying in one place

**instinct** Knowledge of how to do something without being taught

**keratin** The hard substance that forms beaks, hoofs, or nails

**migrate** To move from one place to another when the seasons change

**nesting colony** A group of birds of the same species that nests together

**perch** (n) A branch or other surface on which a bird can rest; (v) to sit on a branch and grip it with feet or claws

**predator** An animal that hunts and eats other animals

**prey** An animal that is hunted and eaten by another animal

**ratite** A flightless bird with a flat breastbone

**soaring** The act of rising upward on warm air currents

**species** A group of very similar living things whose offspring can make babies

**talon** The claw of a raptor

**yolk** The yellow part of an egg that provides food for the growing chick

# Index

7 8 9 0   Printed in the U.S.A.  7 6 5